My First Book About

How Things Grow

Felicity Brooks and Caroline Young

Illustrated by Rosalinde Bonnet

Designed by Francesca Allen

Expert advice from Dr. John Rostron and Dr. Margaret Rostron

Contents

2 Things that grow

4 Plant words

6 All kinds of seeds

8 Spreading seeds

10 From seed to flower

12 Lots of flowers

14 Through the seasons

16 Autumn and winter

18 Growing food

20 Fruits and nuts

22 All about trees

24 Vegetable garden

Usborne Quicklinks

To visit websites with activities and fun facts about plants, go to
www.usborne.com/quicklinks and type in the keywords "how things grow"
We recommend that children are supervised while using the internet.

Things that grow

Things are growing all around us, all the time. Whenever you're outdoors, you're never far from something that's growing. Things that grow are called plants.

Hedges are made of lots of plants growing close together.

Moss grows in shady places.

← moss

Some plants grow by themselves. Some are planted by people.

tomato plant

seeds

petunias

herbs

Herbs are plants that you can eat.

lichen

Lichen often grows on stones.

There are thousands of different kinds of plants in the world. Nearly all of them have green leaves.

Trees are the biggest plants of all.

Use the stickers to add some more plants to the picture.

tree

ivy

Some plants even grow on other plants.

grass

daisies

bush

Bushes are big plants.

rose

geraniums

sunflower

Plant words

Do you know the names of some different plants? Add the sticker pictures to these labels.

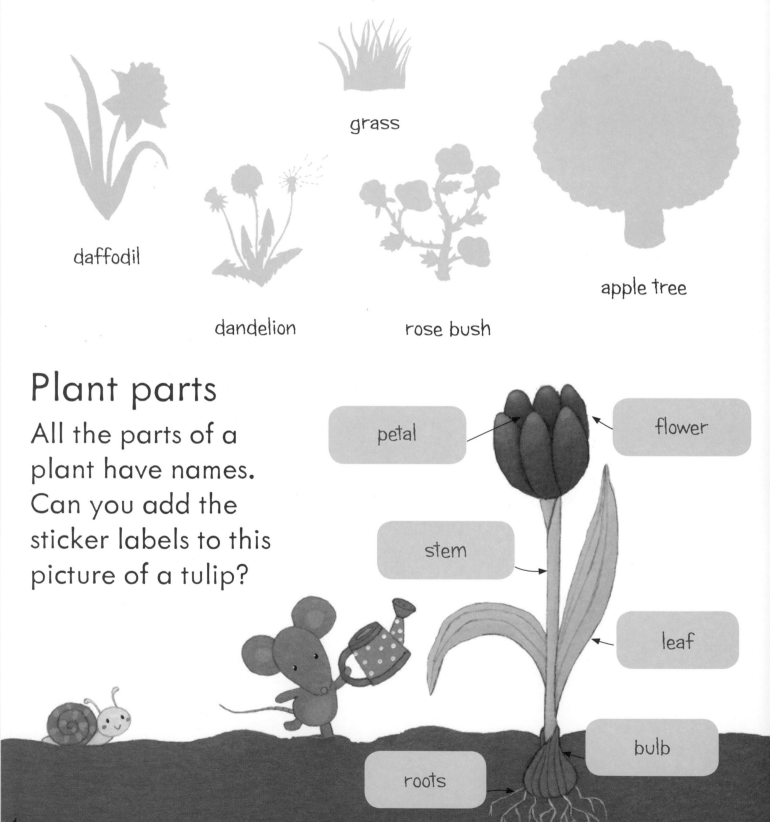

grass

daffodil

dandelion

rose bush

apple tree

Plant parts

All the parts of a plant have names. Can you add the sticker labels to this picture of a tulip?

petal

flower

stem

leaf

bulb

roots

The parts of a tree

The parts of trees have names too. Try adding the sticker labels to these fruit trees.

A tree's flowers are known as blossom.

blossom

branch

leaves

A tree's trunk and branches are covered with a layer of bark.

bark

trunk

fruit

Parts of the blossom turn into fruit.

Roots under the ground hold a tree up.

roots

cherry tree in spring

cherry tree in summer

All kinds of seeds

Most plants start as seeds that come from a parent plant. Some seeds grow inside fruits, cones or nuts. Match the seed stickers to these pictures.

oak leaves

acorn

A little acorn could grow into a huge oak tree.

peach

stone

A peach seed grows in a stone inside the fruit.

tomato

pips

The seeds of tomatoes are little yellow pips.

apple

pips

The pips inside an apple are apple tree seeds.

mango

Big, flat mango seeds grow inside mangoes.

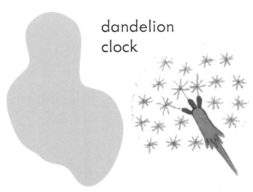

dandelion clock

Fluffy dandelion seeds grow in a dandelion 'clock'.

conker

prickly case

avocado

Avocados have big, heavy seeds inside them.

Horse chestnut seeds (conkers) grow in cases.

pine cone

Pine trees grow their seeds inside pine cones.

See a seed grow

Growing a bean plant takes up to two weeks. It needs water, warmth and light to grow.

You will need: a bean seed, a spoon, water, a glass jar, a sheet of kitchen paper, a big pot with soil in it

Swirl some water in the jar, then tip it out. Fold and roll up the paper and push it into the jar.

Slip the seed between the paper and glass. Put the jar on a warm, sunny windowsill.

Spoon some water into the jar each day. When you have a little plant, plant it in the pot of soil.

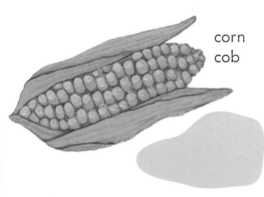

corn cob

Each seed on a corn cob could grow into a plant.

seed head

Tiny black poppy seeds grow inside seed heads.

ear of wheat

Wheat seeds grow in seed heads known as 'ears'.

wing   maple leaf

The seeds of maple trees have little 'wings'.

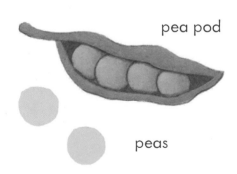

pea pod

peas

Peas and beans are seeds that grow in pods.

strawberry seeds

Strawberry seeds grow all over their parent fruit.

Spreading seeds

Putting seeds where they can grow is called sowing them. People sow seeds in gardens, but wild seeds have ways of sowing themselves.

Seeds may be eaten before they have time to grow.

Some seed pods burst open and the seeds shoot away from their parent plant.

Coconuts can float a long way from their parent tree.

Some seeds drop into water and float to land where they may grow into new plants.

You can blow on a dandelion 'clock' to see its seeds.

Seeds spread by the wind often have 'wings' or little fluffy 'parachutes'.

The sticky seeds fall off when the rabbit scratches.

Some seeds have tiny hooks that catch on an animal's fur as it passes.

Scrumptious seeds

Seeds which grow inside tasty fruits, berries and nuts may be spread by hungry animals.

When a bird eats berries, it eats their seeds too. The bird flies away and the seeds are spread in its poo.

Squirrels often bury nuts to eat later, The ones that they forget about may start to grow into new trees.

How are they spread?

Look at the stickers of groups of seeds. How do you think each group is spread? Add a picture to each label.

Spread by the wind   Eaten by birds   Stick to animal fur

From seed to flower

Once a seed is in a place where it can grow, it needs light, water and time to grow into a plant. If it has these, a plant makes its own food in its leaves.

sunflower seeds

How a flower grows

It takes many weeks for a little seed to grow into a tall sunflower. This shows what happens above and below the soil.

Add the picture stickers to finish these pictures.

rain

soil

1

seed

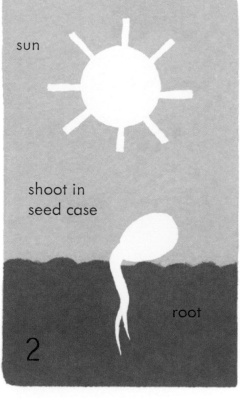

sun

shoot in seed case

root

2

seed leaves

3

seed case

1 If you plant a seed and it has some water, when the soil is warm enough, the seed splits open.

2 A root starts to grow down from the seed. A shoot starts to push up towards the light.

3 The seed case falls off the shoot. Inside it there are baby leaves called seed leaves.

bud

leaf

stem

4

flower

petals

roots

5

seed head

seed

6

4 The stem gets taller, and bigger leaves start to grow. A bud begins to form at the top.

5 The bud opens and a sunflower comes out. Seeds start to form in the middle of the flower.

6 When the petals fall off, a seed head is left. Some seeds fall into the soil and may grow the next year.

Lots of flowers

There are nearly half a million different kinds of flowers in the world. Here are a few that may grow in gardens.

Bees, butterflies and some birds visit flowers to sip a sweet liquid called nectar. Add some of them to the pictures.

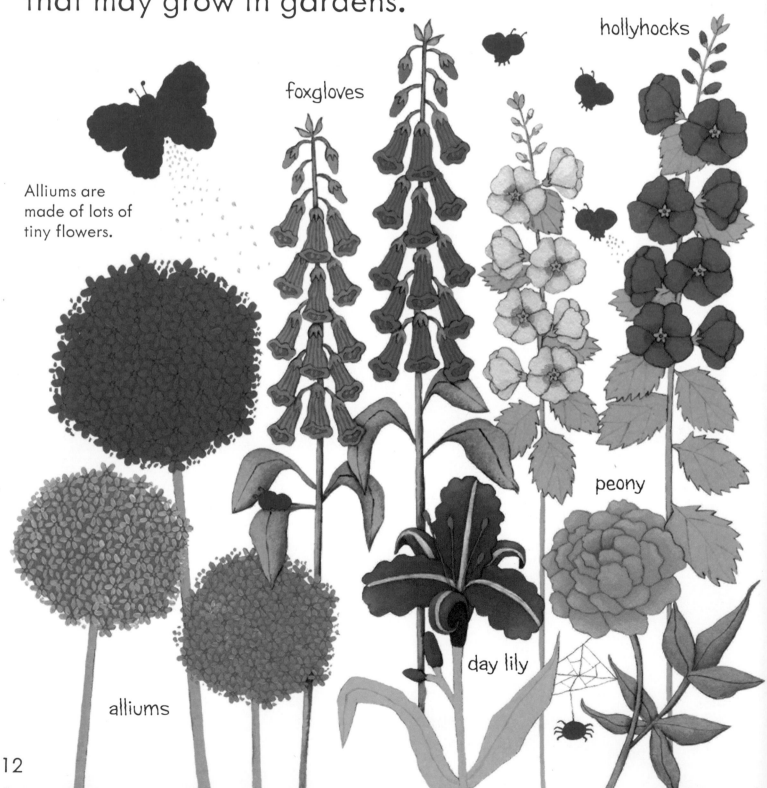

Alliums are made of lots of tiny flowers.

foxgloves

hollyhocks

peony

day lily

alliums

Flowers contain the parts
that will turn into fruits
and seeds.

passion
flower

Passion flowers turn
into passion fruits
with seeds inside.

passion fruit

The life of a poppy flower

bud

A flower starts as a
bud with petals packed
tightly inside it.

petals

The bud starts to open
up and the petals begin
to come out.

poppy
flower

The petals open into a
flower. A seed head
grows in the middle.

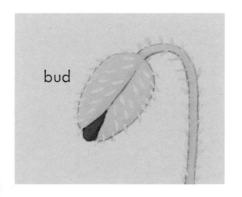

After a few days the
flower starts to die, but
the seeds keep growing.

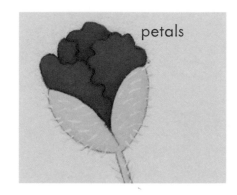

seed
head

When all the petals have
fallen off, the seed head
full of seeds is left.

holes

seeds

When the wind blows,
the seeds fall out of
little holes in the head.

Through the seasons

As the weather changes through the seasons, different plants grow, flower and make seeds.

Spring

When the weather starts to get warmer, leaves and blossom come out on trees. Many flowers grow from bulbs.

cherry blossom

daffodils

tulips

crocuses

Summer

This is the warmest season. All the trees are covered in leaves. Flowers bloom, then fruits and nuts start to form.

willowherb

common poppies

dog roses

ox-eye daisies

wild strawberries

Autumn

As it starts to get cooler, the leaves on some trees turn red, yellow or orange and fall off. Fruits, nuts and berries are ready to eat.

blackberries

apples

chestnuts

mushrooms

Winter

Many trees have no leaves and it's too cold for most plants to grow. Under the ground, seeds and bulbs are waiting for spring.

snow

pine cone

ivy

holly berries

snowdrops

pine tree

17

Growing food

A lot of the food we eat comes from plants. Vegetables are different parts of plants that grow in or under the soil.

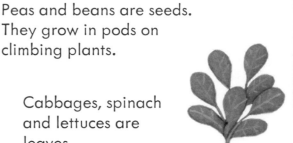

peas

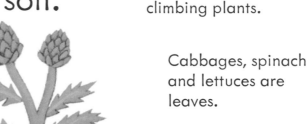

beans

Peas and beans are seeds. They grow in pods on climbing plants.

Cauliflowers, broccoli and artichokes are flowers.

cauliflower   broccoli   artichoke

Cabbages, spinach and lettuces are leaves.

spinach

cabbage

lettuce

Peppers, aubergines and tomatoes grow on leafy plants. They are really fruits.

Some vegetables are stems or stalks.

peppers   aubergines   tomatoes   asparagus   celery

Carrots, beetroot, radishes and turnips are roots.

Potatoes are underground stems called tubers.

carrot   beetroot   radishes   turnip   potatoes

Vegetable competition

Some gardeners like to enter their vegetables into competitions.

Which vegetable should win 'Best in Show'?

Strangest vegetable

Biggest vegetable

Smallest vegetable

Longest vegetable

Use the stickers to show which vegetable you think should win first prize in each group.

Fruits and nuts

All the fruits and nuts that you eat grow on plants, bushes or trees. They form after flowers have bloomed and died.

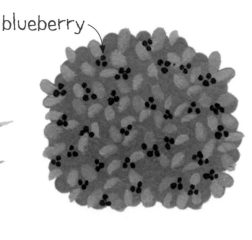

Grapes grow in bunches on plants called vines.

strawberry

Strawberries grow on plants near the ground.

pineapple

Spiky pineapples grow on spiky plants.

blueberry

Many juicy berries and currants grow on bushes.

unripe bananas

Bananas grow in big bunches on a banana tree.

date palm   dates

Bunches of dates grow on a palm tree.

lemon

Oranges and lemons grow on trees too.

How peanuts grow

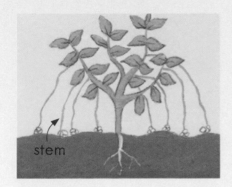

stem

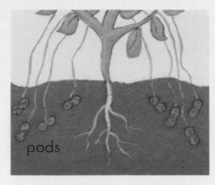

pods

These seeds are peanuts.

After the flowers of a peanut plant die, the flower stems grow down towards the soil.

The stems push down into the soil and hard pods start to form on the ends of them.

Each pod contains two or more peanuts. The pods can be dug up and cracked open.

More tree fruits

The fruits and nuts on this stall all come from trees. Can you add the labels?

apples

peaches

cherries

mangoes

pears

olives

walnuts

plums

All about trees

Trees are the biggest plants of all and live the longest. Some can live for thousands of years.

Losing leaves

Trees that lose all their leaves in autumn are called deciduous trees. Their leaves are mostly soft and flat.

Match the leaf stickers to the names of the trees they come from.

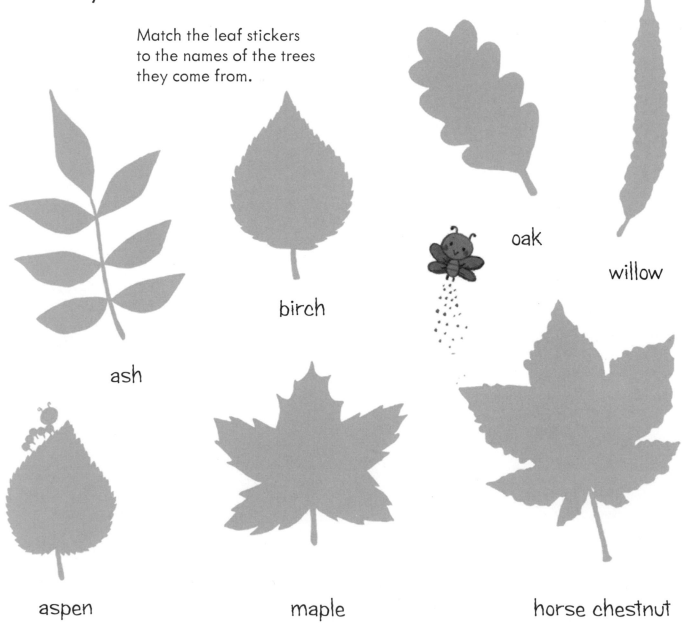

oak

willow

birch

ash

aspen

maple

horse chestnut

Staying green

Trees that stay green all year are known as evergreens. Many have needle-shaped leaves, and seeds in cones.

The world's tallest tree is a redwood named 'Hyperion' in California, USA. At 115m (377ft) it's taller than 20 giraffes.

Pine trees have very long thin needles, and cones.

Spruce trees and fir trees have needle-shaped leaves, and cones.

stone pine

Norway spruce

Holly trees have shiny prickly leaves and red berries.

Laurels have thick leathery leaves and small round fruits.

holly tree

common laurel

coast redwood

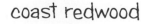

Vegetable garden

All these vegetables are ready to eat. Can you match the picture stickers to the names?

scarecrow

cabbage

cauliflower

broccoli

radishes

lettuce

potatoes

watering can

garlic

leek

carrot

onion

beetroot

Things that grow (pages 2 – 3)

rose

sunflower

geraniums

Plant words (pages 4 – 5)

daffodil

dandelion

grass

rose bush

apple tree

petal

flower

cherry tree in spring

stem

leaf

cherry tree in summer

bulb

roots

Plant words continued (pages 4 – 5)

blossom

trunk

roots

branch

leaves

fruit

bark

All kinds of seeds (pages 6 – 7)

acorn

peach stone

tomato pips

apple pips

mango stone

avocado seed

conker

sweetcorn seeds

poppy seeds

dandelion seeds

wheat seeds

maple seeds

pine seeds

peas

strawberry seeds

Spreading seeds (pages 8 – 9)

maple seeds

dandelion seeds

strawberry seeds

raspberry seeds

burdock seeds

goosegrass seeds

From seed to flower (pages 10 – 11)

1

2

3

4

5

seed head

6

rain

sun

Lots of flowers (pages 12 – 13)

Vegetable competition (page 19)

1st

1st

1st

1st

Best in Show

Fruits and nuts (pages 20 – 21)

| apples | peaches | cherries | mangoes |

| walnuts | plums | pears | olives |

All about trees (page 22)

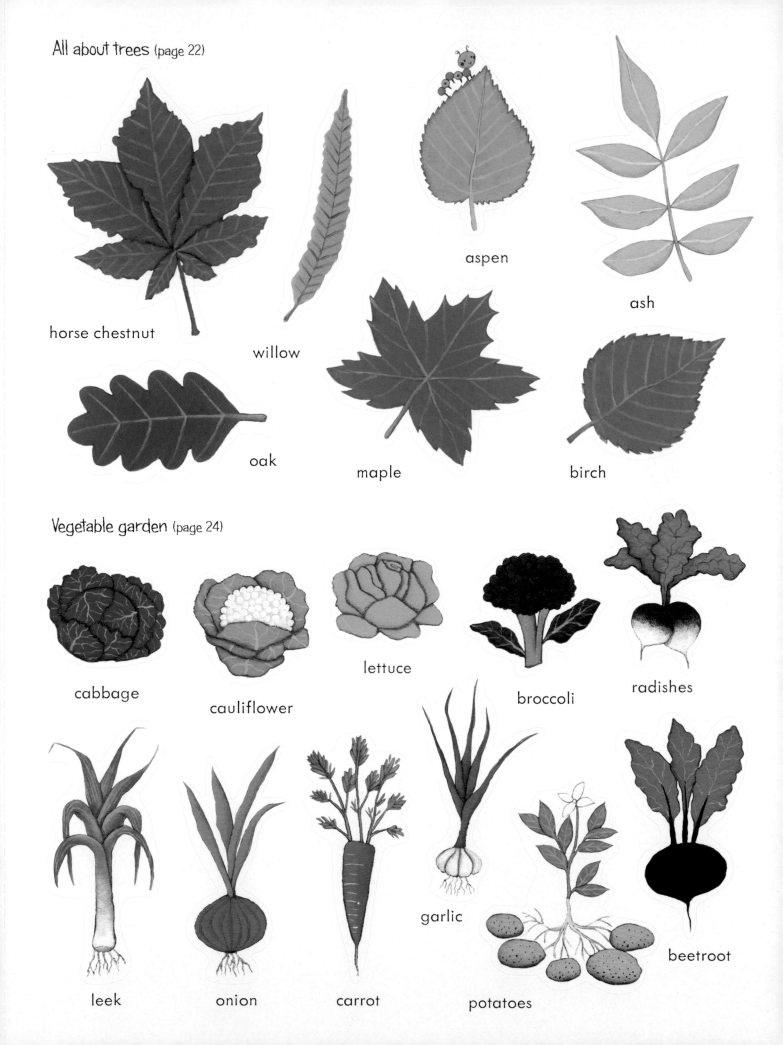

horse chestnut

willow

aspen

ash

oak

maple

birch

Vegetable garden (page 24)

cabbage

cauliflower

lettuce

broccoli

radishes

leek

onion

carrot

garlic

potatoes

beetroot